NOW YOU KNOW

Question
& Answer
Book

WISHING WELL BOOKS®

CONTENTS

HOW DOES IT WORK?

Questions & Answers About How Things Work

By Jack Long
Illustrated by Vern McKissack

Why does a wagon have to be pulled?

For a wagon—or anything—to move, a force is needed. When you pull or push a wagon, your energy is the force that makes the wheels roll over the ground. The harder you pull, or the more force you use, the faster it will go. If you don't pull the wagon, it will not move.

What makes my bicycle go?

The same force that makes your wagon go makes your bicycle go—and that's your energy. The pedals on your bike are connected to a small wheel with teeth called a *gear*. These teeth hold a loop of chain that runs between that gear and another gear on the back wheel. When you push the pedals, the front gear turns. The chain moves and turns the back gear, which turns the back wheel of your bike, and you're off!

ENGINE

GAS TANK

What makes a car go?

You probably know about the engine, the part of a car that makes noise. It is also the part that makes the car go. A car is a very complicated machine. When the driver turns the key, the engine starts. Gasoline mixed with air feeds the engine and keeps it running. The engine makes the wheels turn and that makes the car go.

Why does a boat float?

A toy sailboat bobs along in your bathtub. An ocean liner plows through the waves. Both of these boats float—or stay on top of the water—because they weigh less than the water. That is, the weight of the boat and the space inside it is less than the weight of the water.

What is a submarine?

A submarine is a special kind of boat that can go either on top of or under the water. Submarines are built with lots of empty spaces inside them. When the submarine floats on top of the water, the spaces are filled with air. When the submarine dives underwater, special doors are opened and the air is replaced with seawater. The water is heavier than the air, so it makes the submarine sink under the water.

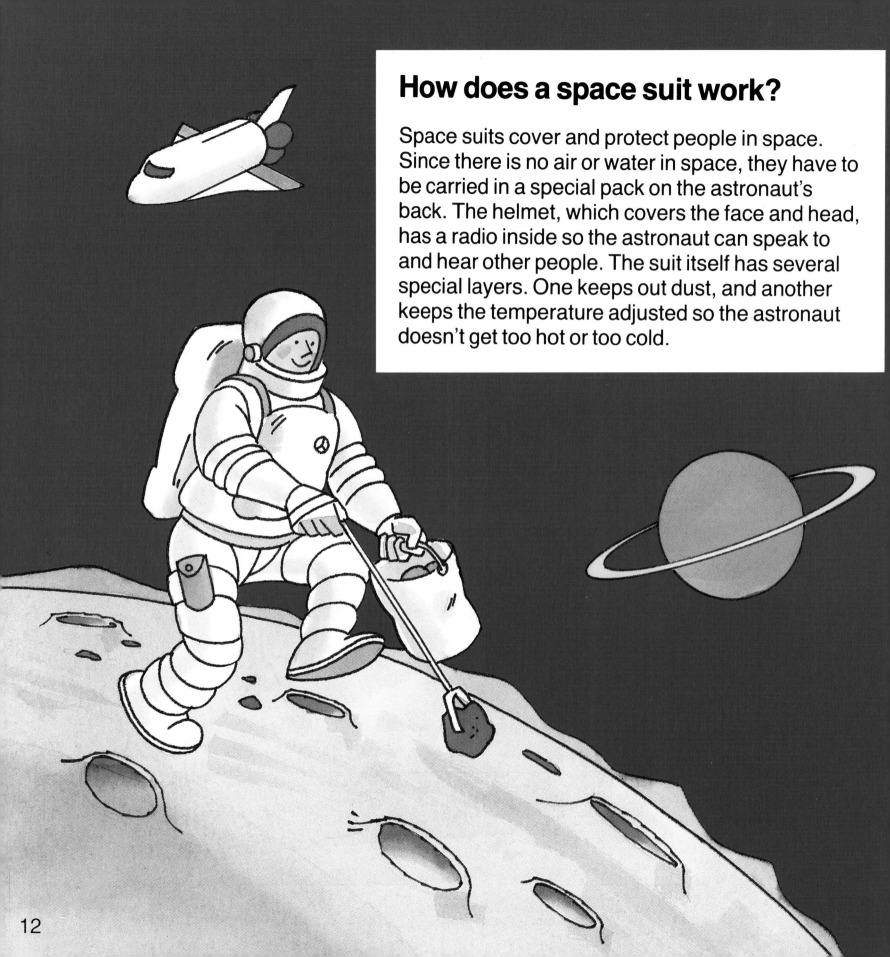

How does a space suit work?

Space suits cover and protect people in space. Since there is no air or water in space, they have to be carried in a special pack on the astronaut's back. The helmet, which covers the face and head, has a radio inside so the astronaut can speak to and hear other people. The suit itself has several special layers. One keeps out dust, and another keeps the temperature adjusted so the astronaut doesn't get too hot or too cold.

How does a refrigerator stay cold?

On a warm day, you reach into your refrigerator for cold juice or some nice, cool yogurt. The refrigerator stays cold because it contains a liquid that *absorbs,* or soaks up, heat. Inside the refrigerator, the liquid moves through pipes to the area where the food is kept. There it soaks up all the heat in the air. Since all the heat is now in the liquid, the air around the food is cool. The liquid travels to another area where a fan cools it off, and it's ready to start the job all over again!

How does a thermometer tell my temperature?

A thermometer tells you how warm your body is. The small glass bulb at the bottom of the thermometer holds mercury, a silvery liquid that *expands,* or takes up more space, when it gets warm. The warmth of your mouth heats the mercury so it moves up the glass tube of the thermometer. The warmer you are, the higher up the tube the mercury goes. The tube is marked with lines and numbers, so you can see exactly what your temperature is. If you are not sick, your temperature is probably about 98.6 degrees.

98.6

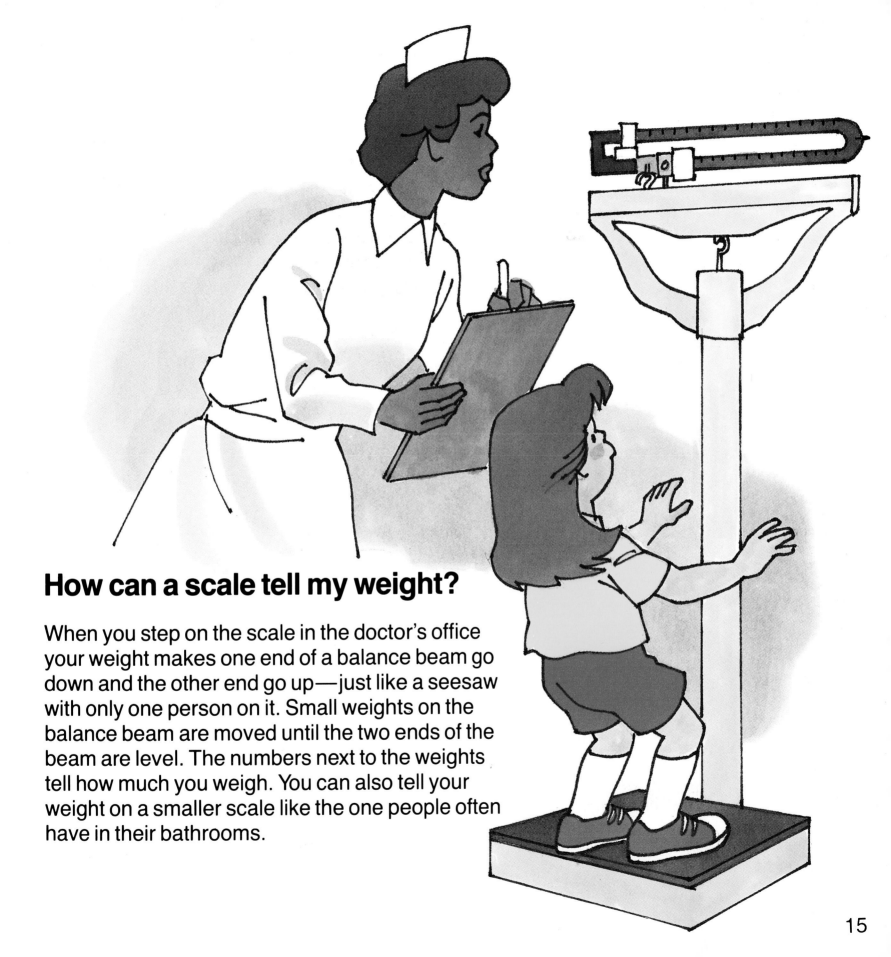

How can a scale tell my weight?

When you step on the scale in the doctor's office your weight makes one end of a balance beam go down and the other end go up—just like a seesaw with only one person on it. Small weights on the balance beam are moved until the two ends of the beam are level. The numbers next to the weights tell how much you weigh. You can also tell your weight on a smaller scale like the one people often have in their bathrooms.

15

What is a magnet?

A magnet is a special piece of metal that can pull other metals to it with an invisible force. When you put two magnets near each other you can feel how strong this force is. A magnet has two ends, or poles, called north and south. The opposite poles of magnets attract each other. If you put the north end of one magnet near the south end of another magnet the two will pull together. If you put the two south ends or the two north ends together, the magnets push apart.

How does a compass work?

Could you find your way back from a strange place? If you knew whether to go north, south, east, or west, you could use a magnetic compass to help you. This kind of compass works because the earth has north and south poles that are powerful magnets. The small needle on a compass is a magnet too. Since the opposite poles of any two magnets attract each other, the earth's north magnetic pole attracts the needle of the compass. The needle, often painted red, points to the north. Now you can head home!

How can I see myself in a mirror?

You know that you can see through a glass window. Like windows, mirrors are made of highly polished glass. But instead of being clear, the back of a mirror is covered with a special silver coating that light cannot go through. When light hits the silver coating, it bounces back at you, and you see yourself reflected in the mirror. Wow, are you cute!

What is electricity?

Everything—air, water, even people—is made up of tiny, tiny parts called *atoms.* Atoms are so small you cannot see them. Atoms have even tinier parts called *electrons.* The electrons have a special power, or charge. Sometimes electrons use their special power to break free from their atoms and move around. Electricity is made when many electrons move in the same direction along a path. Electricity does so many things. It makes the lights go on, it makes your television work, and it even runs your tape recorder!

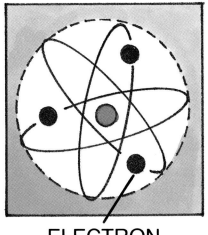

ATOM

ELECTRON

How does a light bulb work?

FILAMENT

Inside a glass light bulb is a frame made of a glass tube, a glass rod, and wires. This framework supports a coil of wire called a *filament.* When you turn on a lamp, electricity enters at the bottom of the bulb and travels to the filament. The filament becomes so hot it glows, giving off the bright light you need to see.

What makes a doorbell ring?

The push button outside your door is connected by wires to the electrical system of your home. When the button is pressed by a visitor, it turns on the electricity. The electrical power makes the buzzer buzz or the bell ring.

How does a key lock a door?

A lock in a door has a metal bolt that slides back and forth when moved by a key. Along the edge of the key is a pattern of small notches. The key's notches fit into the lock like two pieces of a puzzle fit together. When the key is turned, it slides the bolt into a metal plate inside the door frame. Click! Now, the door is locked!

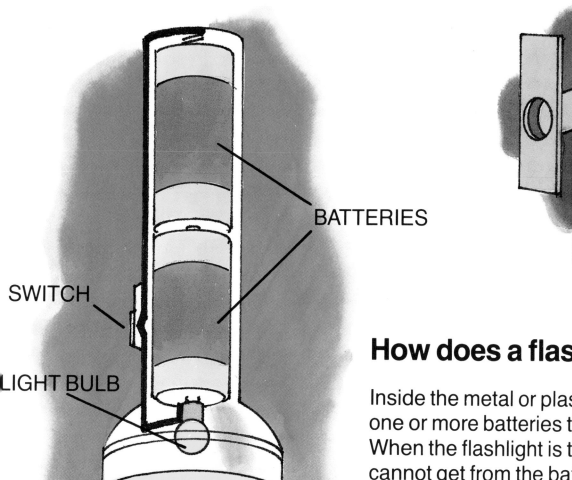

BATTERIES

SWITCH

LIGHT BULB

How does a flashlight work?

Inside the metal or plastic case of a flashlight are one or more batteries that store electrical power. When the flashlight is turned off, the electricity cannot get from the batteries to the bulb. When you switch on the flashlight, you make a path for the power to follow. Electrical power flows from the batteries, through the switch, to the bulb. You then have a small, bright light shining in the darkness!

How does a magnifying glass work?

A magnifying glass is a curved, clear piece of glass called a *lens.* If you hold it close to an object, the lens spreads out the light rays that pass through it. Your eyes see the spread out rays, which make the object appear larger than it really is.

How does a camera take a picture?

With photographs, you can always look at people and places important to you—even if they are far away. The film in a camera has a coating that reacts to light. When you snap a picture, you let light inside the camera. It hits the film, and leaves an invisible picture there. Then, when the film is developed by being placed in a special liquid, the picture you took appears. It is then printed on paper and you have a photograph!

How does a plane get into the air?

Planes use very strong engines to get up into the air. As the plane goes down the runway, it moves faster and faster. The pilot makes the back, or tail, lift slightly. Then, as the plane gains speed, the pilot raises the front, or nose, of the plane. The plane begins to climb as the wind rushes under it. You are in the air—have a nice flight!

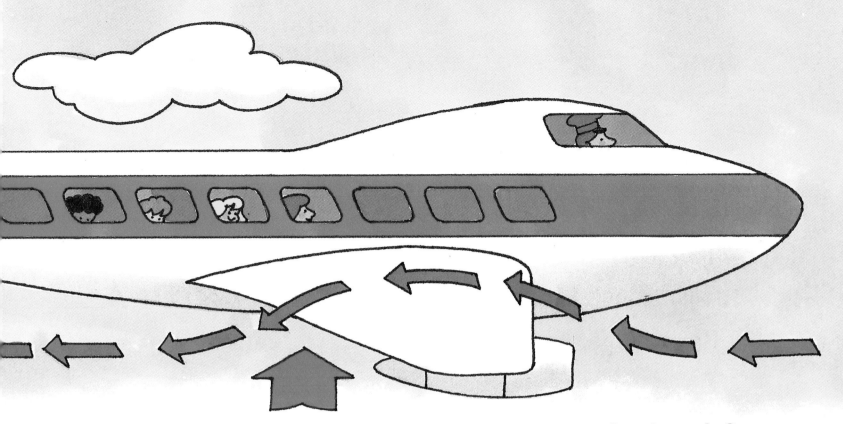

How does a plane stay up in the air?

An airplane's wings are curved on the top so that, when the plane is flying, the air going over the top of the wings moves faster than the air going under them. The air going under the wings is slower but stronger. It pushes up against the wings, lifting the plane and keeping it in the air. The plane is pushed forward through the air by its strong engines.

How does a piano make music?

There is more to a piano than the black and white keys you see. Inside there are more than 200 metal strings stretched from one end of the piano to the other. When you strike a key, it makes a small wooden hammer hit certain strings. That makes the strings move quickly back and forth, or *vibrate*. The vibrating strings make noise, which you hear as music.

Why does a clock tick?

Do you wake up in the morning to the sound of a ringing alarm clock? The power for one kind of clock comes from a metal coil called a *mainspring*. The mainspring's movement is controlled by a set of large and small gears (wheels with teeth). As the edges of two of the turning gears catch together, you hear *tick-tock-tick-tock*.

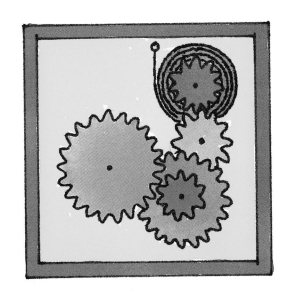

How does a radio work?

At a radio station music and voices are sent out into the air
as invisible electrical signals. Your radio uses electric paths,
or *circuits,* to pick up the signals out of the air and turn them
back into words and music. It then plays them loud enough
for you to hear.

How does television work?

Television is a combination of pictures and sound. The picture you see begins with a television camera. This special camera uses light and electricity to see and hear. It turns the picture and sound into a series of electrical signals. These signals are then sent by an antenna or cable to your television, which changes them back into what you see and hear. Most of the time, the picture and sounds are stored on tape, and then played back later for your television. That is why you can see the same show more than one time.

Why does a balloon float?

For a balloon to float in the air, it must weigh less than the air around it. Balloons that float are often filled with *helium*. Helium weighs less than the air around us, so the balloons float. If you blow up a balloon yourself, it will not float because your breath is the same weight as the air.

What makes my kite fly?

A kite is a very light plastic or wooden frame covered with paper, plastic, or cloth. A long string is attached to one end. If you stand with your back to the wind and hold up the kite, the wind will pick it up and carry it into the sky. The force of the wind keeps the kite going higher and higher in the air. Hold on tight to the string or the kite will blow away!

How does a telephone work?

A telephone has two main parts. The part you speak into is called the *transmitter.* The part you listen to is called the *receiver.* When you talk into the transmitter, it turns your words into electrical signals. It then sends them over wires to another phone. That phone uses its receiver to change the signals back into words again. Since all telephones have both a receiver and a transmitter, you can talk to anyone on any other telephone!

How does a vacuum cleaner work?

An electric motor inside a vacuum cleaner turns a fan. The fan pushes air out of the vacuum cleaner. Air from the room rushes in to take its place. The air that rushes in carries dust, dirt, and small objects. They are stored in a disposable paper bag that fits inside the vacuum cleaner.

Why does popcorn pop?

Popcorn is made from dried kernels of corn. When you heat the corn, tiny drops of water inside the kernels turn into steam. The steam wants to escape, but it can't. The only way for it to get out is to break open the kernel. When the kernel pops, you have popcorn!

Why does soda fizz?

Whether you call it soda, pop, or tonic, soda pop is a mixture of water, sugar, salt, flavorings, and a special kind of air called *carbon dioxide*. The fizz you see is tiny bubbles of carbon dioxide. When a bottle or can of soda is opened, all the bubbles rush to the top. You see all the bubbles as fizz. Sometimes those tricky little bubbles can even pop up and tickle your nose!

How is a record made?

By now, you know that sounds can be turned into electrical signals. To make a record, music and voices are turned into electrical signals. Then, those signals are fed into a machine that turns them into a series of wavy grooves that are imprinted on a plastic disc. Many, many copies are made of that disc. We call one of those copies a record.

How does my record player work?

The needle on the tone arm of your record player reads all the grooves on a record, and turns them back into electrical signals. The record player turns those electrical signals into sounds and words again, and makes them loud enough for you to hear.

How does a tape recorder work?

Tape recorders have two wheels, or reels, of tape, which store electrical signals. In a cassette recorder, both of those reels are inside the plastic case. The tape recorder does two things. It makes the tape move from one wheel to another. It also changes words into electrical signals and changes those signals back into words. When you *record* a voice or music, the machine puts signals onto the tape. When you *play* a tape, the recorder reads the signals and changes them back into words and sounds for you to hear.

HOW DO I GROW?

Questions & Answers About the Human Body

By Robert Carola and Barbara Shook Hazen
Illustrated by Mel Crawford and Lynn Sweat

What are the different parts of my body?

Your body is separated into different parts that do different things. You have a stomach that helps you eat, drink, and go to the bathroom. You have lungs for breathing, and bones and muscles that help you to stand up straight and move around. You have a heart that pumps blood that carries food and air to all the different places in your body, and you have skin that holds all the parts together. And in charge of it all, is your brain. That's quite a body you've got there!

What does my brain do?

Your brain, which is very nicely protected inside your head, is like a special "control center." As well as thinking, it also helps you see, hear, talk, sleep, grow, and lots of other things. In one way or another, your brain takes care of almost everything your body does.

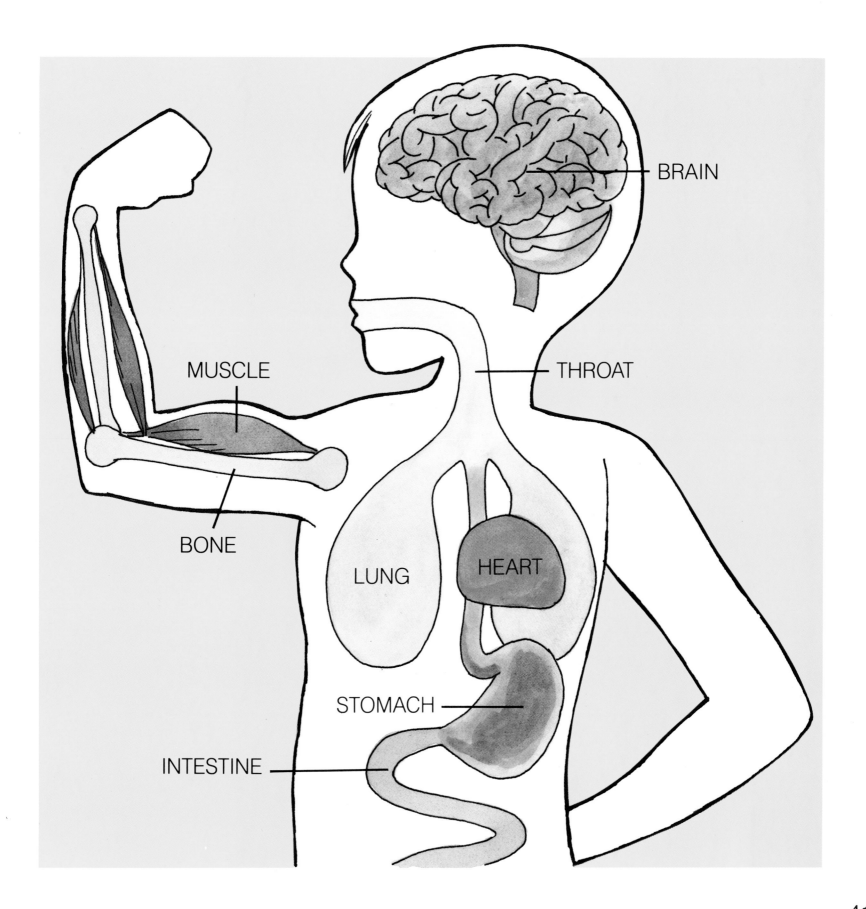

BRAIN

THROAT

MUSCLE

BONE

LUNG

HEART

STOMACH

INTESTINE

41

Why do I get hungry?

When you get hungry, it's your body's way of telling you that it needs a fresh supply of food. Your body uses food to get energy, to grow, to fix worn-out parts, and to do lots of other things that you don't even have to think about.

What happens to my food when I eat it?

Two things happen to your food when you eat it. First, it is chopped up into small pieces when you chew, and then it is churned up even more when it reaches your stomach. Special juices in your mouth and stomach also help to make small pieces. When all the food is mixed up and softened, it is pushed out of your stomach. Then, your blood carries it to the parts of your body that need it. When you go to the bathroom, you are getting rid of the parts of the food that your body doesn't need.

What happens when food "goes down the wrong way"?

Almost always, your food goes down a tube that leads to your stomach. The breathing tube next to the food tube is usually shut off while you swallow. But sometimes a little bit of food or water gets into the breathing tube—it "goes down the wrong way." When that happens, you begin to cough without even thinking about it, and before you know it, the breathing tube is clear, and you can get back to your meal.

Why do I get thirsty?

Your skin, muscles, blood, and all the other parts of your body contain a lot of water. When you get thirsty, it's your body's way of telling you that it's getting too dry. You get thirsty for lots of reasons. Maybe you haven't had a drink in a long time, or you ate some very dry food or salty food like potato chips. Or, perhaps you are thirsty from singing your favorite song for a long time without stopping.

Why do I burp?

When you swallow your food, you may also swallow some air, especially if you eat too fast. That air has no place to go, so it comes up again, and you "burp." Sometimes you burp a little while *after* you eat, when gas comes up as you are digesting your meal. People usually think burping is rude, so it's nice to say "excuse me" after a loud burp!

45

What do my lips do?

Like your tongue, your lips help you to eat your
food and to talk. Your lips can open and close to let
food and air in, or they can close tight to keep water
out when you go swimming. What are some other
things you can do with your lips? Here are three:
You can pucker up to whistle, you can blow out
your birthday candles, and best of all, you can kiss
your family goodnight. Lips are *really* important.

Why do my teeth have different shapes?

You have different kinds of teeth because they do different kinds of chewing. The sharp ones in front are called *incisors*. They are good for nibbling and tearing food like corn on the cob. The big flat teeth in the back, called *molars*, are used for crushing and grinding food like peanuts. You never even have to think about which ones to use. Your teeth just seem to know when to go into action!

Why do I have to brush my teeth?

You should brush your teeth after meals and at bedtime to wash away germs and the food that gets stuck between your teeth. Some of those germs can even use sugar to make your teeth sticky, so that *more* food sticks to your teeth! If you don't brush the food and germs away you might get cavities, little holes in your teeth that will have to be fixed by a dentist.

What do my fingers do?

Your fingers can do so many different things! The most important thing they do is to hold things. Because you have fingers you can draw with a crayon, hold a glass of milk, or imitate a crawling spider. You can also shake hands with your friends, throw a ball, or point at a beautiful butterfly. What else can your fingers do?

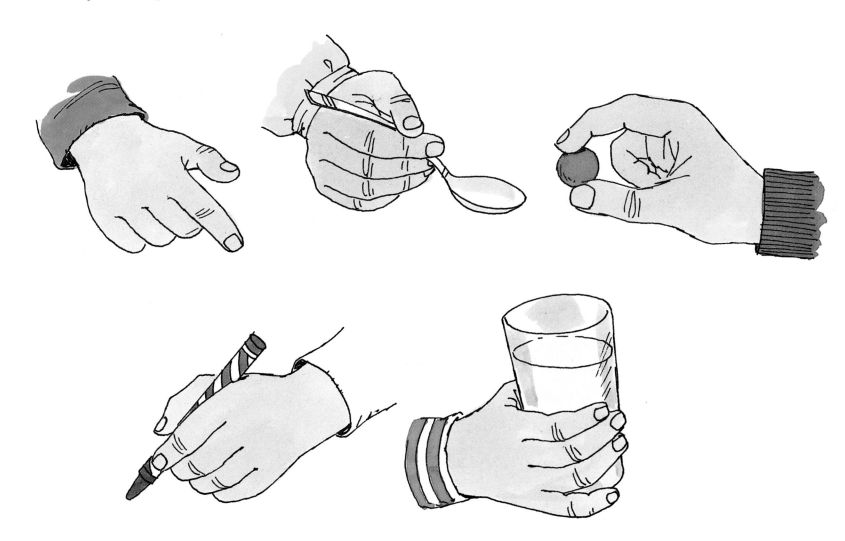

Why do my fingers look like raisins when I stay in the bathtub too long?

When you stay in the tub a long time, your fingerprints soak up a lot of water—just the way a paper towel picks up a spill. When you get out of the tub, the water in your fingertips leaks out through tiny little openings in your skin. Some of the water that was in your fingertips *before* you took a bath comes out too. So your fingertips look a little wrinkled for a while—just like raisins!

Why are my fingerprints different from anyone else's?

Your fingerprints (the tiny lines on your fingertips that you can hardly see) began to form even before you were born. There are so many different ways for the lines to loop and twist that there is no chance that your fingerprints will be exactly like anyone else's. Your toe prints, and the prints of the bottoms of your feet and the palms of your hands, are also different from anyone else's.

What do my toes do?

Because you have toes, you can stand up without falling over, and you can walk and run as fast as you do. And besides, toes are fun to wiggle in the sand!

Why do my shoes get too small?

Your shoes get too small because you are still growing. The muscles, bones, skin, and all the other parts of your feet (and the rest of you too) will probably keep growing until you are about 21 years old. But you do most of your growing while you are still a child. Sometimes you grow fast (like when you are a teenager), and other times you grow more slowly (like right now).

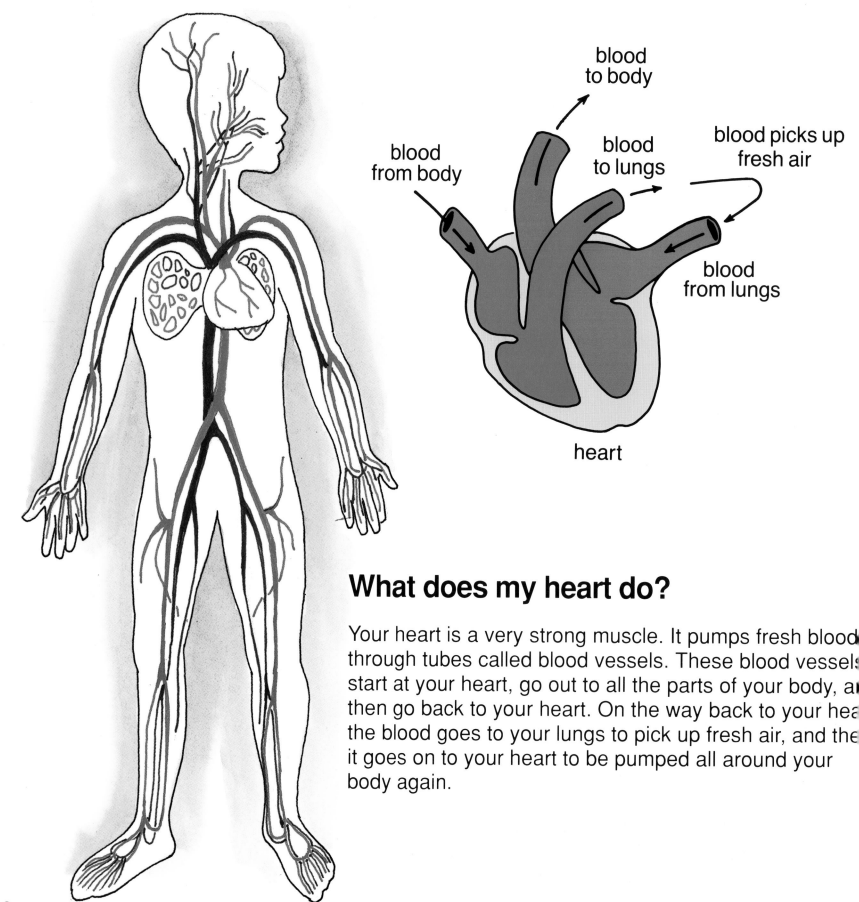

blood
to body

blood
from body

blood
to lungs

blood picks up
fresh air

blood
from lungs

heart

What does my heart do?

Your heart is a very strong muscle. It pumps fresh blood
through tubes called blood vessels. These blood vessels
start at your heart, go out to all the parts of your body, and
then go back to your heart. On the way back to your heart
the blood goes to your lungs to pick up fresh air, and then
it goes on to your heart to be pumped all around your
body again.

What does my blood do?

Blood does so many things that it's hard to tell about all of them. But here are some of the important things blood does. When you breathe in, your blood carries the fresh air to all the different parts of your body. While your blood is making the trip, it picks up the stale air in your body and carries it back to your lungs so you can breathe it out. Blood also carries little bits of digested food to all the parts of your body that need it. Blood helps to keep you from getting sick too. It has its own special parts called *antibodies* that keep germs from spreading. And these are just *some* of the things blood does!

Why does my heart beat faster when I run?

When you run, your muscles use up a lot of air in a hurry. You breathe faster to take in extra air. Then your heart beats faster to send the blood carrying that extra air to your muscles.

Why does blood look blue under the skin of my hands and wrists?

The blood you can see in the little tubes in your hands and wrists is on its way back to your heart and lungs to pick up some fresh air. Blood that isn't carrying much fresh air looks a little blue. Blood with a lot of fresh air looks red. That's why your lips and your cheeks look pink. The blood under the skin there has lots of fresh air in it.

Why does a small cut stop bleeding?

Special parts of your blood have a very important job. As soon as you start bleeding, they work together to make a plug that makes the bleeding stop. The plugging is called a *blood clot*. Sometimes, the clotted blood dries on your skin and makes a scab. Try not to pick at a scab—you may start bleeding all over again. Putting a bandage on a cut helps to close the cut and keeps germs from getting inside.

Why do I have hair?

Hair looks nice, especially when you wash and comb it, but most of all, hair protects you. The hair on your head helps to keep you warm in the winter and cool in the summer. It also protects your head against bumps. Your eyebrows act like little cushions to protect your eyes, and they also cut down the glare of the sun and keep sweat from running into your eyes. Eyelashes are like little screens that keep dust and other things out of your eyes. How about the really tiny hairs on your arms and legs? Those hairs are too small to keep you warm or protect you from getting bumped, but they are really good at letting you know when a bug is crawling on you!

Why is some hair straight and some hair curly?

Each hair on your head comes out of a tiny opening in the skin of your head. A round opening makes the hair straight. An egg-shaped opening makes the hair wavy, and a wiggly-shaped opening makes curly hair. The kind of hair opening you have is passed on to you from your parents. What kind of hair do you have?

Why doesn't it hurt when I get my hair or nails cut?

The part of your hair and nails that shows is not alive, so there is no feeling when you get a haircut or trim your nails. The part that is alive is mostly under your skin.

Why do I shiver and get goose bumps?

Shivering and goose bumps are ways your body helps you to stay warm. When you get chilly, your brain sends a message to tiny muscles under your skin. Some of those muscles pull up the little hairs on your skin, causing small bumps. We call them goose bumps, since they look a little like a goose's skin. Your brain tells some other tiny muscles to just jiggle around a bit. All that jiggling makes you shiver. The jiggling muscles give off heat, and that helps you stay warm. Shivers and goose bumps don't work as well as a cup of hot chocolate, but they're a start!

Why do I sweat?

The purpose of sweating is to cool you off when you get too hot. Sweat is made in little compartments under your skin. When you get really hot, the sweat is sent up to your skin through tiny openings. Once the sweat gets on your skin, it begins to evaporate—it disappears into the air. But the sweat needs heat to evaporate. Where does the heat come from? From your skin! And, as your skin loses heat, you feel cooler.

Why are there different colors of skin?

Of course you know that paints come in different colors. The thing that gives paint its color is called pigment. Your skin has pigments, too. The dark pigment that gives your skin most of its color is called *melanin*. The more melanin there is, the darker your skin is. A yellow pigment called *carotene* also adds to the color of your skin. The thickness of your skin also has something to do with its color. Thin skin lets a little more of the reddish color of the blood underneath show through than thick skin does.

What does my skin do?

Your skin protects the inside of your body from dirt, germs, and other things you don't want to get in. It holds all your pieces together, and even gives you something to tickle and scratch.

Why do I have to wash my face?

If you look very closely, you can see that the skin on your face (and every place else on your body) has tiny openings called *pores* that look like little dots. It's very important to keep these openings clean by washing your face, otherwise they can get clogged up and cause skin problems such as pimples.

What do my bones do?

Bones hold up everything in your body and, because they are attached to your muscles, they also help you move. Without bones you couldn't even make a fist to knock on the door!

How many bones do I have?

When you were born, you had about 300 bones, but some of them are already joining together as you grow. By the time you are a grown-up you will have 206 bones.

Which is my smallest bone?

Your smallest bone, called the *stapes,* is inside your ear, along with two other ear bones almost as small. It is also called the *stirrup* because it is shaped like the stirrups you put your feet into when you ride a horse. These three tiny bones inside your ear help you to hear.

Which is my longest bone?

Your thighbone (the one that connects your knee to your hip) is your longest and strongest bone. It is called the *femur*.

What do muscles do?

Because your strong muscles are attached to your bones, they make your bones move. And when your bones move, *you* move too. It may be hard to believe, but you have over 600 muscles! Some are very small (the smallest ones are inside your ear), but they all help your bones to move so you can walk, run, jump, hop, twiddle your thumbs, and even hear!

Why do I hiccup?

There's a big muscle in your chest that helps you breathe. Sometimes that muscle gets tired and doesn't work as well as it should for a minute or two. When that happens, too much air goes into your chest, and a little trap door in your throat snaps shut to try to stop more air from coming in. The sound of the little door shutting and the extra air stopping is the noise we call a hiccup. Don't worry though, you'll stop hiccupping in a couple of minutes.

Why do I cough?

Sometimes you cough when you are sick and your throat is sore. Usually, though, a cough is your way of getting rid of something that's in your throat but doesn't belong there. If a piece of food gets stuck, or if little bits of dirt get into your throat, you blow them out by coughing. It's a good idea to cover your mouth so you won't cough on other people.

Why do I sneeze?

Sneezing is a lot like coughing. It can happen when you have a bad cold, but there are also other reasons why you sneeze. When dust, your cat's hair, or something like that gets in your nose, a special alarm goes off that makes your nose tickle—and guess what? You sneeze, "A-choo!" Bless you!

A-choo!

What is a fever?

When your mother takes your temperature by putting a thermometer in your mouth, she is trying to find out how hot the inside of your body is. Usually, if you are not sick, your temperature is about 98.6 degrees. If you're not feeling well, your body may be hotter than that. When that happens, we say you have a "fever." Usually, the higher your temperature is, the sicker you are. But, in a couple of days, your fever should go down and you will feel better.

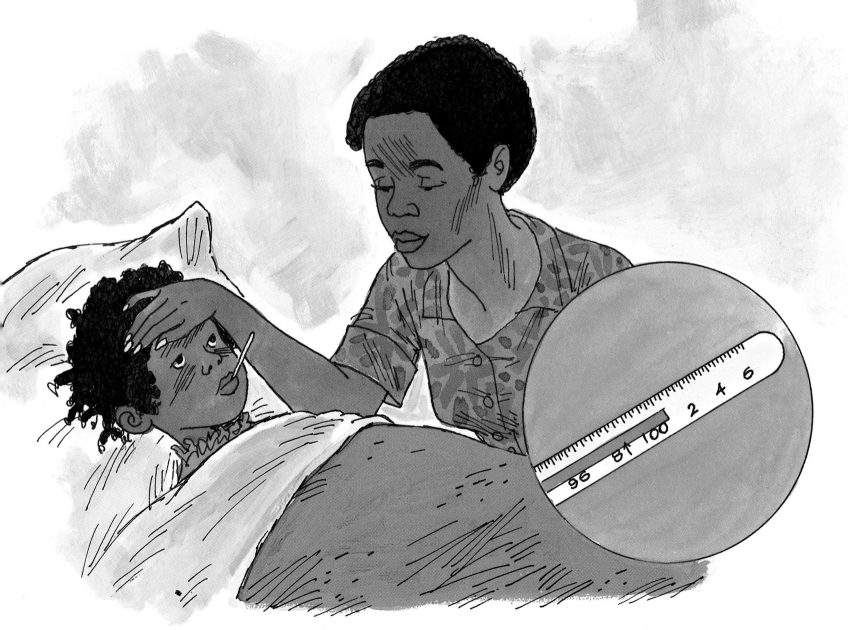

Why do I yawn?

When you are tired, you may not breathe as deeply as you usually do, so your body tries to make up for it by taking a big gulp of air all at once. *That's* a yawn. Don't forget to cover your mouth!

Why do I get tired?

You usually get tired when you play or work very hard and your body needs some rest. You also get tired—or sleepy—when it's time to get to bed, so that your *whole body* can get some rest. You need lots of sleep—at least eight hours a night—to grow up healthy and strong. If you get a good night's sleep, then you'll be able to play hard again tomorrow.

Why do I get out of breath?

You get out of breath when you play or work very hard, and you use up more air than you breathe in. You'll be fine once you stop to rest for a few minutes and slowly breathe in some fresh air.

What is an *allergy?*

For some reason, your body gets fooled by things in the air, like dust, or by certain foods. Your body acts as if those things could harm you and it sends out chemicals to protect you. These chemicals may make you act or feel funny—you might start to sneeze, get a rash, or have a runny nose for a little while. It means you are allergic to that particular thing. But allergies happen only once in a while. Most of the time your body knows exactly how to take care of itself every step of the way as you grow up. Isn't your body wonderful?

What are feelings?

Feelings make you the special person you are. They make your life richer and more interesting. Feelings are what make you happy when a friend comes to play, sad when it's raining and you can't go outside, and proud when you tie your shoes all by yourself.

Do feelings show?

Feelings show in what you say and do. Hugging your family shows that you love them. Waving and shouting "hello" shows that you are glad to see a friend. Some feelings show on your face. When you're happy, you smile; when you're sad, you may frown. If you're surprised, your eyebrows may raise and your eyes open wide.

Why do I feel sad?

You feel sad when something you don't like happens. You may feel sad when you're not allowed to do something you want to do, when your dog is sick, or when you lose a favorite toy.

Poor Spot, I hope you feel better soon.

What can I do for someone who's sad?

Try to find out why the person is sad. Sometimes you can help best just by listening or by being there and letting the person know you care.

Why do I feel happy?

Things that you like make you happy. Eating something yummy, receiving a present, playing with a friend, or visiting your grandparents are all things that might make you happy. Different things make different people happy. Can you think of some things that make you happy?

Why do I feel happy when I make someone else happy?

When you do something that makes someone else happy, you feel good about yourself. If it's someone you care about, it makes you happy when that person is happy.

Why do I feel different ways different days?

Feelings change, just like the weather. Many things combine to make you feel the way you do, from what happened yesterday to something someone said to you. Sometimes even the weather affects how you feel.

Does my body have anything to do with how I feel?

Yes, if you have a cold or a headache, you might feel tired or grumpy. If you had a good night's sleep, you'll probably feel wide awake and full of energy.

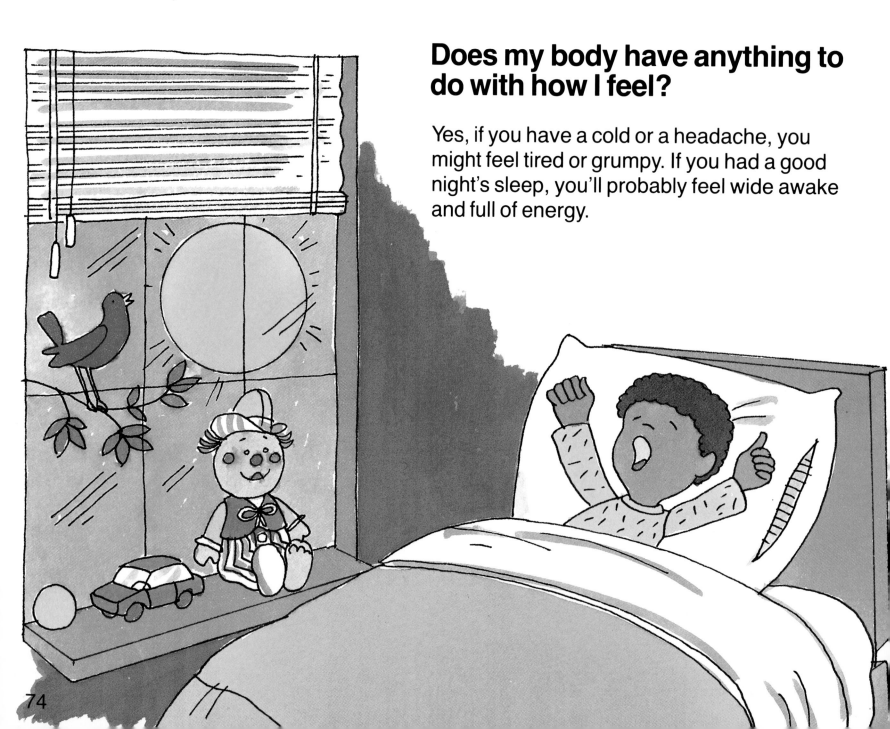

What should I do if I'm mad at someone?

Don't keep your anger bottled up inside you. You need to talk to the person and tell them why you're angry. If you're too upset to talk calmly, wait awhile until you've cooled off, then talk.

What should I do when I'm mad at myself?

Forgive yourself and try to do better next time.

Why is it important to like myself?

The way you feel about yourself influences the way others feel about you. If you treat yourself with affection and acceptance, others will most likely treat you the same way.

WHY IS THE SKY BLUE?

Questions & Answers About Nature

By Jack Long
Illustrated by Vern McKissack

Why do cats purr?

Cats, from pet kittens to lions, purr to say "hello" or to show they are happy. A cat purrs by narrowing its voice box, or *larynx*. This disturbs the air flowing in and out of the cat's lungs as it breathes. The sound of the air going in and out is what we hear as a *purr*.

How do parrots talk?

Parrots do not really talk the same way people do. Parrots talk by imitating or repeating what you say to them. If you say the same word over and over again to a parrot, it will copy you. Once the parrot has learned a word, it can say the word whenever it wants to. Smart birds often pick up words on their own.

Why does a rattlesnake rattle?

A rattlesnake has loosely jointed rings at the end of its tail. When the snake wants to warn away its enemies, it coils up and shakes its tail. The rings hitting each other make a rattling sound.

How do grasshoppers hop?

Animals move in many different ways. They run, jump, crawl, fly, swim, and hop. A grasshopper has strong back legs, which enable it to hop as far as twenty times its own body length. With its wings spread out, a grasshopper may glide even farther.

How does an earthworm crawl?

An earthworm is made up of many parts, or segments. Each segment has its own muscles and two stiff bristles on the bottom that can grip the soil. To move, the worm stretches the front segments forward, making them longer and thinner. Then the worm pulls up the rear segments, making them shorter and fatter. The worm inches forward by stretching and shortening over and over again.

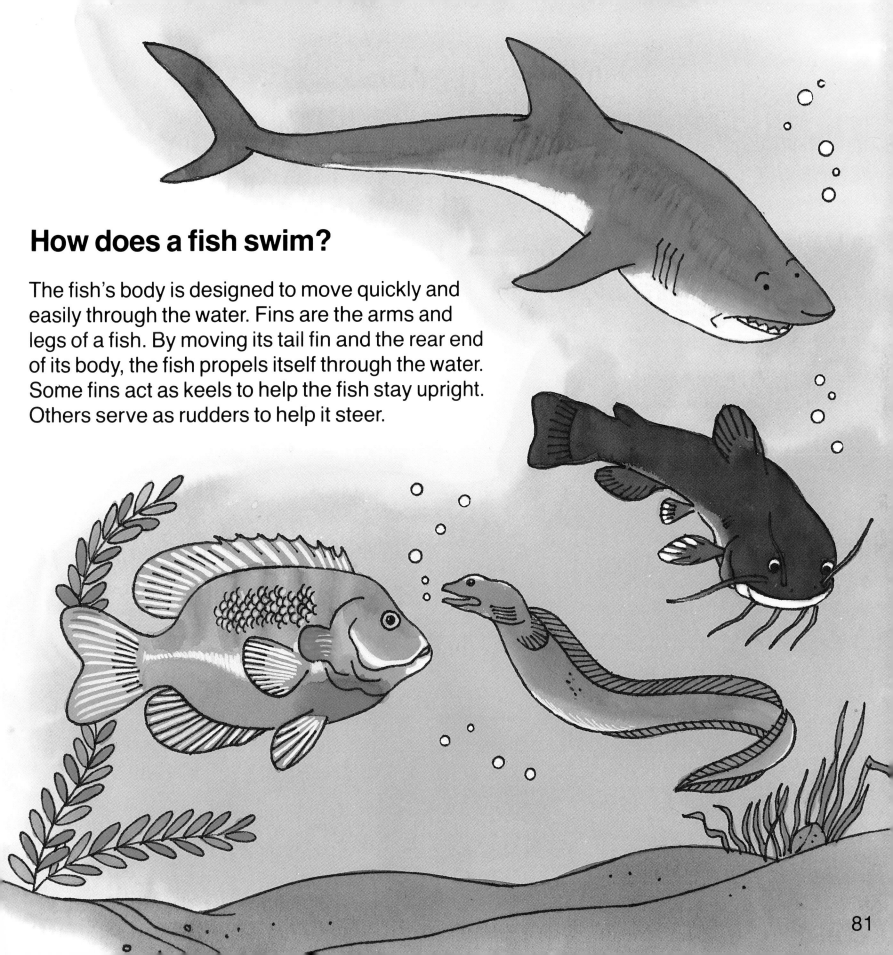

How does a fish swim?

The fish's body is designed to move quickly and easily through the water. Fins are the arms and legs of a fish. By moving its tail fin and the rear end of its body, the fish propels itself through the water. Some fins act as keels to help the fish stay upright. Others serve as rudders to help it steer.

Why can birds fly?

Birds are perfectly built for flying. They are strong but lightweight. A bird has large chest muscles to pull its wings up, and smaller chest muscles to pull them down. As the bird moves forward through the air, there is less pressure above the wings than there is below them, so the bird rises—just like an airplane. The tail feathers help the bird to steer.

How does a baby bird hatch from its shell?

Just before a baby bird hatches, it starts to roll around inside its eggshell. It takes slow breaths and begins to cheep. Then the bird uses a special tooth on the end of its bill to peck a hole in the egg. It slowly chips a groove all the way around the top of the eggshell. A special neck muscle helps the bird to push the shell off, and out it steps!

82

How do birds know when to migrate?

Many birds *migrate,* flying south every fall and north again every spring. Birds know it is time to migrate when the days get shorter, the weather gets cooler, and food becomes harder to find. In preparation for their long trip south, they eat large amounts of food to store fat. The migration instinct is so strong that some birds start their journey on almost the same date every year.

How do bees make honey?

A bee sips a sweet liquid called *nectar* from a flower, stores it in his body, and flies back to the hive, which is made of honeycomb. The nectar is stored in a cell of the honeycomb. Other bees fan the cell with their wings to evaporate the water in the nectar. After about three days, the nectar has become honey, which the bees seal with wax and store in the comb for winter.

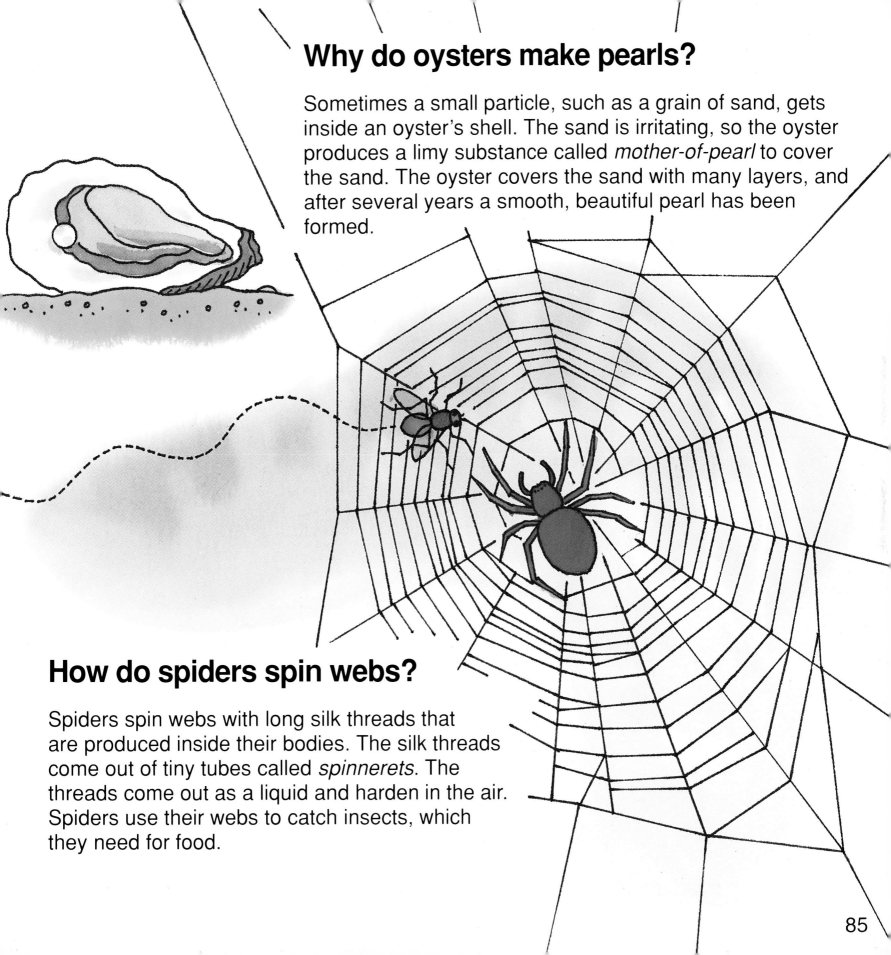

Why do oysters make pearls?

Sometimes a small particle, such as a grain of sand, gets inside an oyster's shell. The sand is irritating, so the oyster produces a limy substance called *mother-of-pearl* to cover the sand. The oyster covers the sand with many layers, and after several years a smooth, beautiful pearl has been formed.

How do spiders spin webs?

Spiders spin webs with long silk threads that are produced inside their bodies. The silk threads come out of tiny tubes called *spinnerets*. The threads come out as a liquid and harden in the air. Spiders use their webs to catch insects, which they need for food.

Why are there clouds in the sky?

As the sun warms the water on ponds, lakes, rivers, and oceans, invisible drops of water, called *water vapor,* rise into the air. When the air carries the vapor high into the sky, it cools. As the water vapor cools, it changes, or *condenses,* into water droplets and ice crystals, which we see as a cloud. Fog is simply a cloud near the ground.

Why does it rain?

The tiny water droplets in clouds bump into each other and combine to form bigger drops. As the drops grow larger, they becomes too heavy to stay in the air, and fall as rain.

Why does it snow?

The water in clouds can behave in unusual ways. Sometimes, the water vapor in clouds freezes into tiny, tiny ice crystals. As more and more vapor freezes, the crystals grow into delicate snowflakes which fall to earth as snow.

87

What causes lightning?

The water droplets that make up clouds have charges of electricity that are either positive (+) or negative (−). When a group of droplets with a positive charge meets a group of droplets with a negative charge, they make a spark, or flash of electricity, that we see as lightning. A flash of lightning can jump between groups of droplets in the same cloud, between different clouds, or between a cloud and the earth.

What causes thunder?

Lightning is very hot. When it flashes through the sky, it heats up the air immediately around it. This hot air moves so fast that it bumps into the colder air nearby, and the result is a clap of thunder. Thunder is nothing more than a loud noise.

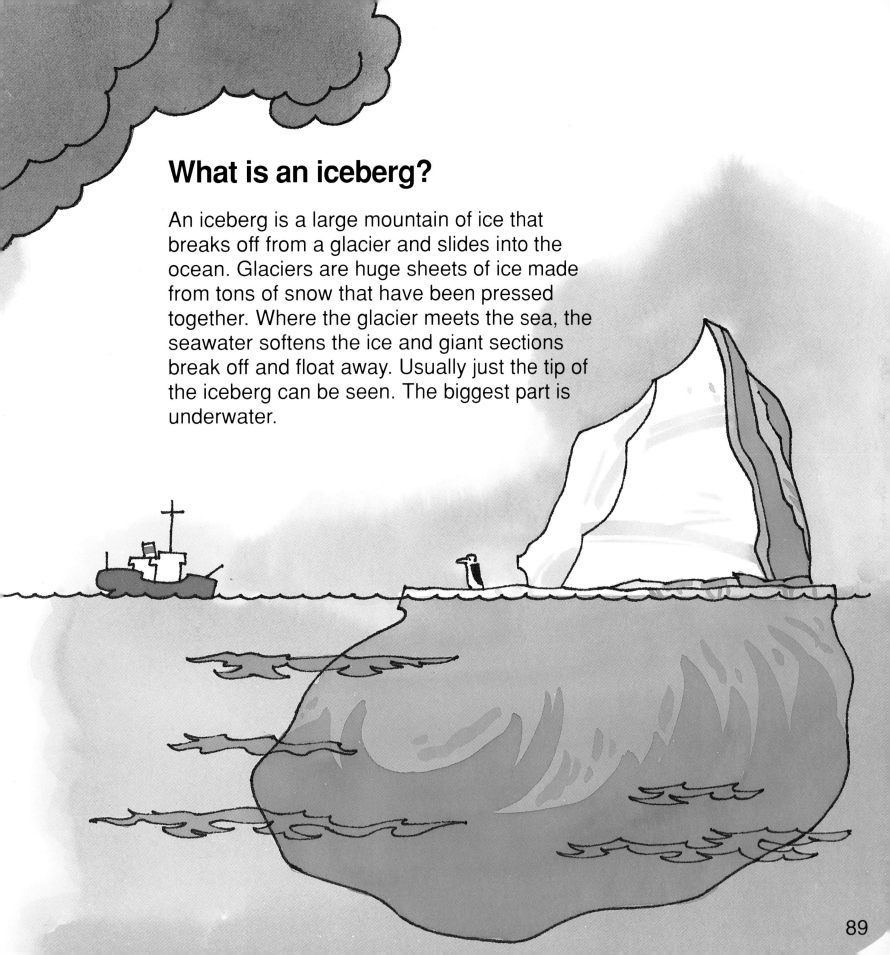

What is an iceberg?

An iceberg is a large mountain of ice that breaks off from a glacier and slides into the ocean. Glaciers are huge sheets of ice made from tons of snow that have been pressed together. Where the glacier meets the sea, the seawater softens the ice and giant sections break off and float away. Usually just the tip of the iceberg can be seen. The biggest part is underwater.

89

Why does the wind blow?

Energy from the sun warms the air around the earth, making it expand and rise. As the warm air rises, cooler air nearby moves in to take its place. This constantly moving air is wind. Wind is also affected by things on the earth's surface, such as mountains, deserts, and oceans.

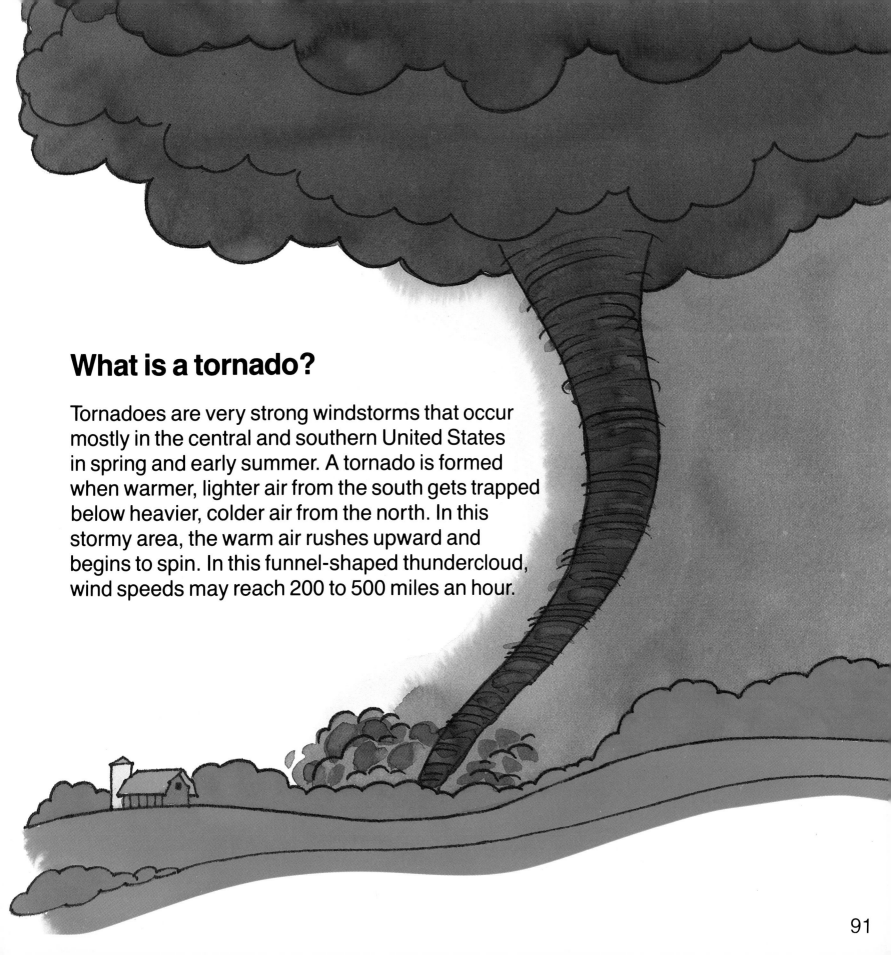

What is a tornado?

Tornadoes are very strong windstorms that occur mostly in the central and southern United States in spring and early summer. A tornado is formed when warmer, lighter air from the south gets trapped below heavier, colder air from the north. In this stormy area, the warm air rushes upward and begins to spin. In this funnel-shaped thundercloud, wind speeds may reach 200 to 500 miles an hour.

What is fire?

Fire is the intense heat and light that comes from burning something. A fire needs three things to burn—fuel, like wood; oxygen from the air; and a temperature high enough to make the wood burst into flames. Fire is very important. It cooks our food, keeps us warm, and provides energy to run machines.

What is a volcano?

The center of the earth is very hot. In some places it is so hot that the rock melts. The melted rock finds a weak spot in the earth's crust and pushes toward the surface. When it breaks through, or *erupts*, it forms a volcano. The volcano, which looks like a mountain, is made from the melted rock that has cooled and hardened.

Why is there day and night?

Although you can't feel it, the earth is continually spinning. Every day it makes one complete turn on its *axis,* an imaginary line that runs from the North Pole to the South Pole. When the part of the earth you live on faces the sun, it is light outside. This is day. When that part of the earth turns away from the sun, it becomes dark. This is night.

DAY   NIGHT

Why are there different seasons?

At the same time that the earth is turning on its axis, it is also moving in a path around the sun. When the part of the earth you live on is closest to the sun, it is warm and sunny. These seasons are spring and summer. When that part moves away from the sun, the days become shorter and colder. This is fall and winter.

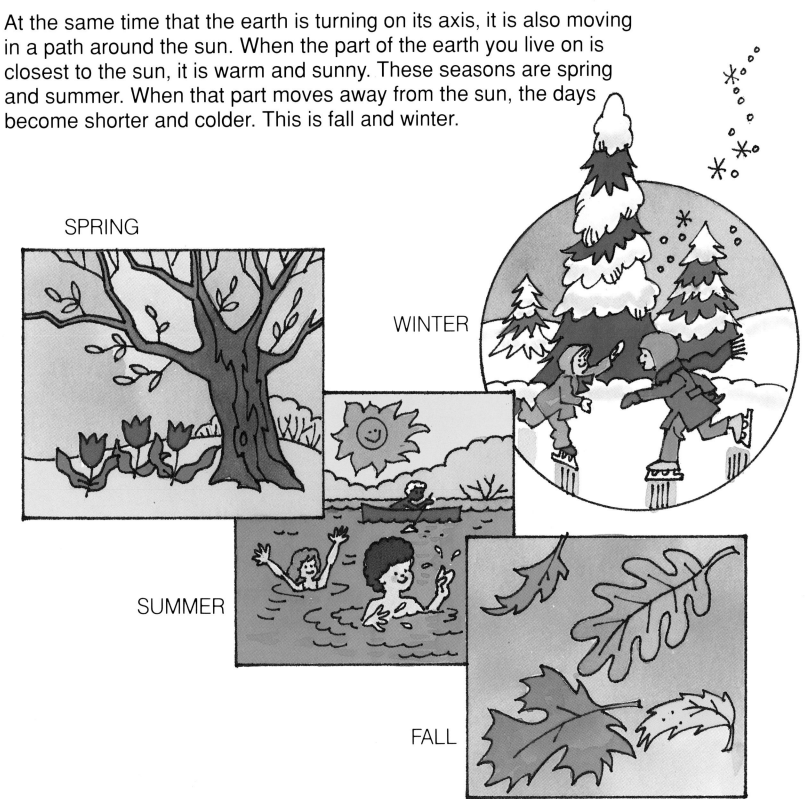

SPRING

WINTER

SUMMER

FALL

What is a desert?

Deserts are large, dry, sandy areas of the earth that receive little or no rain. One of the biggest deserts is the Sahara in Africa. Because of the Sahara's location, the air above it contains very little water. There are no clouds or rain. Deserts are so dry that very few kinds of plants and animals can live there. Camels are one of the few animals that can make the long trip across the desert without getting thirsty.

What is a jungle?

A jungle is a forest located in a warm climate where there is a lot of rain. The combination of warm weather and moisture makes a perfect place for all kinds of plants and trees to grow. Also called a rain forest, the jungle is home to many different animals, including tigers, monkeys, snakes, lizards, birds, and butterflies.

Why do stars twinkle?

Stars are suns, like our own. They shine all the time. You can't see stars during the day because our own sun is so bright. But if you look at the sky on a clear, dark night, you can see thousands of them. Starlight has to travel through miles and miles of space. When the light hits the air that surrounds us, which is called the *atmosphere,* it breaks up and scatters. This makes it look as if the stars are twinkling.

What are shooting stars?

A light streaks across the night sky. This flash of light is called a *shooting star* or *meteor.* Shooting stars are really parts of a comet that have entered the earth's atmosphere and travel very fast. When they enter our atmosphere, they heat up and glow, and then burn out.

Why does the moon change?

The moon travels around the earth just like the earth travels around the sun. The moon has no light of its own. What we see in the sky at night is the light from the sun reflected off the moon's surface. The moon seems to change size and shape because, as it travels, only a part of the sunlit half can be seen from the earth.

How are mountains formed?

Mountains are formed in many different ways. Most are made by movements of the earth's crust. Cracks, or *faults,* cause huge blocks of rock to tip up or drop down. In other places, underground pressures force the earth's crust into long lines of wavelike folds.

What causes earthquakes?

The earth's crust is made up of enormous, rocklike plates. Usually these plates fit together like pieces of a puzzle. Sometimes heat or other strong forces deep inside the earth cause the plates to move. When these huge plates move, it makes the earth above shake.

How does a seed grow?

A seed contains a tiny plant with a small stem, a root, and leaves. The seed also contains a small amount of food to feed the plant as it begins to grow. Once it is planted in the soil, the seed needs light from the sun, moisture from the rain, and oxygen from the air in order to keep growing.

Why do plants need roots?

Roots anchor a plant in the ground and help it stand up. They reach into the soil for minerals and water, which the plant uses for food.

LEAVES

STEM

SEED

ROOTS

Why do flowers bloom?

Flowers bloom to make seeds that will grow into new plants. When a plant produces a flower, the bright colors and the pleasant smell attract insects, like bees and butterflies. The insects drink the flower's nectar. As they go from flower to flower, they carry the flower's *pollen,* or seed dust, with them. Flowers need pollen from other flowers to make seeds which will grow into new plants.

Why is grass green?

Grass, like other plants, is green because it contains a green coloring called *chlorophyll*. Chlorophyll helps plants change sunlight into food and energy. Because of the chlorophyll, plants like grass need only water and carbon dioxide from the air to make their own food.

Why do leaves change color in the fall?

Leaves really contain many colors. In spring and summer, we see mostly green because of all the chlorophyll that is working to make food for the plant. In the fall the leaf stops making food and the green chlorophyll disappears. Then we can see the other colors in the leaf, such as red, yellow, and gold.

Why is the ocean salty?

Even though the water in lakes, streams, and rivers doesn't seem salty, there is salt in it. This water eventually empties into the ocean, carrying the salt along with it. When water evaporates from the surface of the ocean, the salt stays behind. This has been going on for thousands of years so that now the water in the ocean is very salty. Swimming in the ocean is fun because the salt in the water helps you to float.

Why is the sky blue?

The color of the sky depends on the atmosphere, the air above the earth. The atmosphere is made up of many gases such as *oxygen* and *carbon dioxide*. When the rays of the sun, which are made up of many different colors, shine through the atmosphere, they are separated and scattered. Blue light is scattered the most, so the sky appears blue on sunny days.

What makes a rainbow?

Sunlight is made up of seven different colors. When the light hits a drop of water, it is bent and split into its seven colors. If sunlight falls on many drops of water, usually right after it rains, the rays form an arch of the seven colors in the sky. This is a rainbow.

SUNLIGHT

HOW DO I KNOW?

Questions & Answers About the Senses

By Robert Carola
Illustrated by Mel Crawford

What are my senses?

Your senses are all the parts of your body that tell you what's happening around you. For instance, you see with your eyes, hear with your ears, feel with your skin, taste with your tongue, and smell with your nose. All of your senses work together with your brain to let you know what's going on outside your body.

What controls my senses?

The control center of all your senses—taste, smell, sight, hearing, touch, and balance—is your brain. For example, your eyes let light into your body, but it is your brain that actually figures out what you are seeing. Sometimes our brains are compared to computers, but that's not really so. Your brain is much smarter than a computer!

How many different colors can I see?

If you have a large set of crayons or colored markers, you're used to seeing a lot of colors. But you can see more shades of colors than you ever dreamed you could. Your eyes can tell the difference between thousands and thousands of different shades of colors!

Why do some people wear glasses?

Inside your eye is a part called the *lens*. It changes shape when you are looking at things very close (like when you read a book) or far away (like when you recognize a friend a block away). Some people, even children, have eyes whose lenses don't change shape very well. They have to wear eyeglasses, which have special lenses, so that they can see clearly.

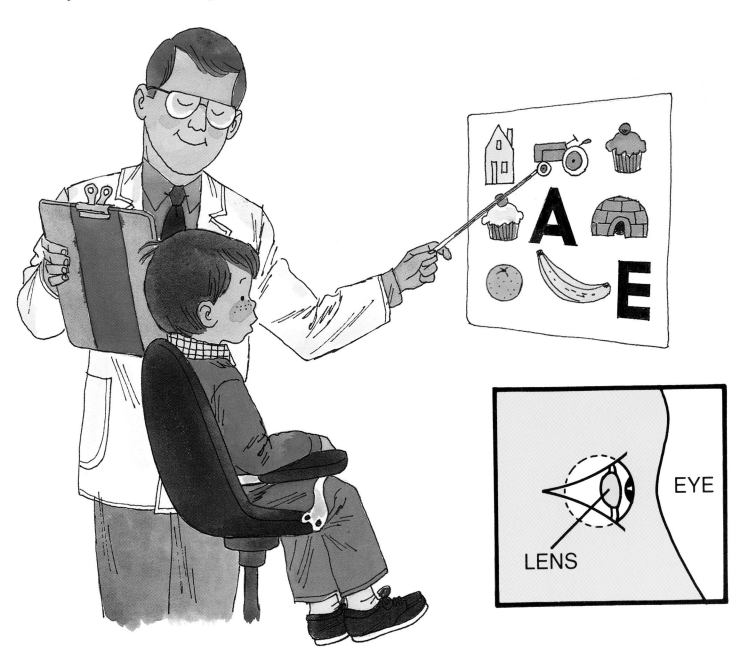

Why is the color of some people's eyes different from the color of other people's eyes?

Children usually have the same eye color as one of their parents or grandparents. Eye color is something you *inherit,* which means it is passed on from parents to their children. The darkness or lightness of eyes comes from something called *melanin.* The more melanin you have, the darker your eyes will be. Melanin also gives color to your skin and hair.

What eye color do most people have?

Most people have dark-colored eyes, usually brown. Those same people usually have dark-colored hair. People with blue eyes tend to have light, or blond, hair. What color are your eyes?

How can I see in the dark?

Look in the mirror and you will see a black dot in the middle of your eye. It is called the *pupil*. It gets bigger to let in more light, or smaller to let in less light. When you walk into a dark room, your pupils open wide to let in a lot of light. At the same time, special parts of your eyes called *rod cells* also help you to see in the dark. When you've been in a dark room for only a minute, you can already see ten times better than when you first walked in. After 40 minutes in the dark, you can see as well as you're going to.

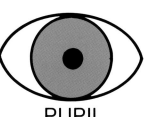

PUPIL
IN THE LIGHT

PUPIL
IN THE DARK

Why does it bother my eyes to look at snow on a sunny day?

On a sunny day the bright sunlight bounces off the white snow, making the light even brighter. It usually takes a while for your eyes to become comfortable when you look at something that bright. To protect their eyes from the strong light, people often wear sunglasses when they go skiing or to the beach.

Why do my eyes make tears sometimes?

You know that when you cry you make tears, but there are also other times your eyes tear. When smoke gets in your eyes or when you help Mom chop an onion, your eyes may make tears. These tears help to keep your eyes clean, and to make them feel better when something bothers them.

Why do I blink my eyes?

You blink your eyes every few seconds without thinking about it. Every time you blink, a special liquid that looks like water runs across your eyes. It washes away little bits of dirt, kills germs, and keeps your eyes clear, wet, and smooth. Blinking keeps your eyes clean and healthy.

What is an optical illusion?

An optical illusion is something that tricks your eyes. You think you see one thing, but another thing is really true. For instance, which of these red lines do you think is longer?

The top one *looks* longer, doesn't it? But it's a trick. Both red lines are the same.

Here's another optical illusion. Which line is longer, the red or the black? You probably said the black line is longer, or maybe you figured out that it only *looks* longer. Actually, both lines are the same.

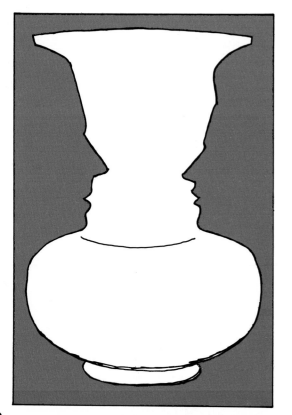

Another kind of optical illusion uses shapes instead of lines to fool your eyes. Do you see a vase or two faces? Or maybe you see both pictures? Sometimes an artist can make two different things out of one picture.

Why can something look two different ways?

Sometimes your brain helps you imagine that one thing looks like something else. Have you ever looked up at the clouds and thought you saw a face, an animal, or something else? Your eyes see a cloud, but your imagination turns it into an elephant.

What is braille?

Since they cannot see, blind people use *braille* to read and write. Braille is a way of showing letters and numbers as raised dots that can be felt with the fingertips. The dots are like a special code that blind people learn to understand.

Do people with big ears hear better?

The part of your ear that is important for hearing is *inside* your ear, where you can't see it. The size of the outside part of your ear makes no difference in how well you hear.

Do I hear better than grown-ups do?

Yes, you do. In fact, babies usually hear the best of all, so let's not make any really loud, scary noises if there's a baby in the room. Most grown-ups don't hear as well as children do. As people get older, some of the tiny parts inside their ears may not work as well as they used to. If you take very good care of your body, your hearing probably won't change very much when you're a grown-up.

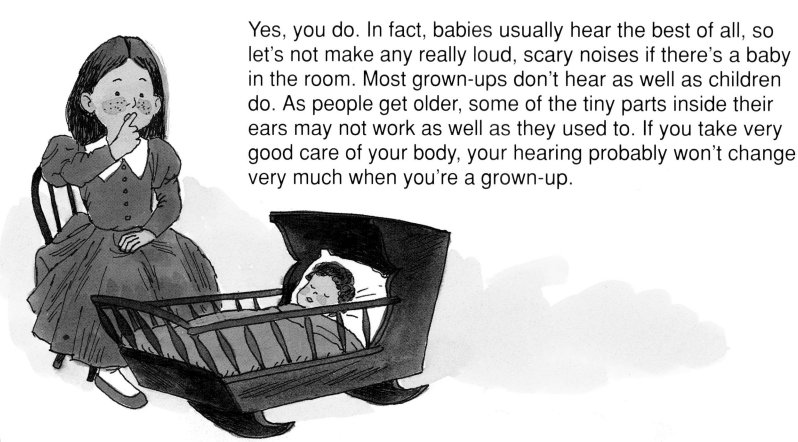

Are loud sounds bad for my ears?

Very loud sounds, if they last for a while, can harm the delicate parts inside your ears that help you to hear. People who work near airplanes at an airport, or who work with noisy machines, wear special ear coverings to protect their hearing.

Why do children's voices sound smaller than the voices of adults?

Inside your throat are folds of skin called *vocal cords*. We don't have to think about it, but we make sounds by pulling the vocal cords together and letting air from the chest come up and pass over them. Your vocal cords are shorter and thinner than a grown-up's vocal cords, so your voice sounds smaller than a grown-up's voice.

Why do I sound different on tape?

When you listen to yourself talk, your voice is changed a little bit. Some of the sound you are hearing is carried through the bones of your head. It's almost like when your voice sounds louder in an empty room. When you hear yourself on tape, your voice is carried only by the air, and it sounds the way it always sounds to other people.

Why do I get dizzy sometimes?

You usually get dizzy when you spin around quickly, and then suddenly stop. When you stop, a liquid inside your ear keeps moving. The moving liquid makes you feel like you are still moving, but in the other direction. Your brain gets a little mixed up by all this, and you feel dizzy for a little while.

Why do my ears "pop"?

The *eardrum* is a thin piece of skin between the inner and outer parts of your ear. Usually the force of the air pressing on your eardrum is equal on both sides, and you can't feel it. But when you're in an airplane that's taking off or landing, or in an elevator in a tall building, the air pressure on the outer side of your eardrum may change all of a sudden. That change makes your ears "pop." By swallowing or by opening your mouth wide, you can help to make the air pressure on the inner side of your eardrum equal to that on the outer side.

What does my tongue do?

Your tongue does lots of things. It has little bumps on it called "taste buds." They allow you to taste the difference between salty food, like potato chips, and sweet food, like candy or ice cream. Your tongue helps you to chew your food by moving the food to where your teeth can bite it. After your food is all chewed up, your tongue helps to push it down your throat to your stomach. And here's something very important about your tongue—it helps you to talk. Just try to say "hello" or "good-bye" without moving your tongue!

Do I taste food better than grown-ups do?

You certainly do taste food better than grown-ups do, because you have more taste buds that work. As you get older, some taste buds get worn out and don't work anymore.

Why does my mouth water when I see something good to eat?

The watery liquid in your mouth is called *saliva*. Because saliva is so important in helping you digest your food, you start making extra saliva (your mouth begins to "water") as soon as you see or smell something good to eat. By the time you actually start eating the food you have plenty of saliva ready to do its job!

Why can't I taste food when I have a cold?

When you taste food, you are actually tasting it *and* smelling it at the same time. If you can't smell your food, you can't taste it either. Try holding your nose and eating a piece of food. Can you taste it? If you have a cold, you probably have a stuffy nose too, and you can't taste your food very well because the "smellers" in your nose are blocked.

How many different smells can I smell?

Your nose is amazing—it can smell about 4,000 different smells! You probably have only three or four favorites. Perhaps it's the smell of freshly baked cookies, just-mowed grass, or your mother's perfume. What is your favorite?

Why does my nose run when I cry?

You know that when you cry, tears flow out of your eyes. But they may also slide down a tube that goes from inside your eyes to your nose, and that makes your nose begin to run. That's why some people need to blow their nose when they cry.

What is my "funny bone"?

If you have ever bumped the "funny bone" near your elbow, you know it's not funny! In fact, it's not even a bone. What we call the funny bone is really a nerve. We call it "funny" because it tingles when we bump it.

Why does my foot "fall asleep" sometimes?

Sometimes when you cross your legs for a while, you keep the blood from reaching your foot and your foot feels numb. When you uncross your legs and let the blood go through again, you may get a tingly feeling. Why? All the little nerves that "fell asleep" because they didn't get enough blood are now waking up. You can almost feel them "waking up" and stretching.

Why do I get itchy sometimes?

You feel itchy, and you want to scratch, when something very light and delicate touches your skin. Tiny "feelers" in your skin called *nerve endings* send a message to your brain, and you usually end up scratching. You might also feel itchy if you have a bug bite or a rash.

Why does hot feel different from cold?

You have special nerve endings in your skin for hot or cold, light touch or heavy touch, pain, itch, and tickle. If you touch something hot, then the "hot" nerve endings send a message to your brain. If you touch something cold, then it is the "cold" nerve endings that send the message. When your brain gets the message, then you know exactly what you are touching!

Why do I use my fingertips to touch and feel things?

There are many special nerve endings in your fingertips that let you touch and feel things—even very small things. As good as your fingertips are at feeling things, they are not the best touchers and feelers in your body. Can you guess what part of your body is the best "toucher" and "feeler"? It's the tip of your tongue!

Why do I get a headache sometimes?

There are many reasons why you might get a headache. Headaches sometimes happen when you have a cold or are not feeling well. Sometimes your eyes get tired, maybe from watching too much television, and you get a headache. Or you may get a headache that's mostly in your forehead and cheeks. That's usually a *sinus* headache. Sinuses are little empty spaces inside your head that can get infected, or that can hurt when the weather changes suddenly. It's best to rest when you have a headache.

Why can't babies talk?

Learning to talk takes time. Babies have to listen for a long time before they can copy what they hear. When they are first born, babies cry to let you know they want something. By their first birthday, they can say a few simple words. They learn to say many words and even simple sentences by the time they are two years old.

Why do I get sleepy?

Sometimes you're so busy or you're having such a good time that you don't even realize you're getting tired. But sooner or later, your brain always lets you feel sleepy so you'll know it's time to go to bed. Sleep is one of the most important things your body needs, and your brain helps you to stay healthy by making sure you get enough rest.

How do I know when to wake up?

If you go to bed when you are supposed to, and you're not sick or more tired than usual, you will probably wake up all by yourself in plenty of time to have breakfast. How do you do that? Everybody needs a different amount of sleep to keep healthy (grown-ups need less than you do), and your brain "knows" when you've had enough sleep. When it's time to wake up, your brain sets off a special alarm that only you can feel, and you wake up.

Do I move around while I'm asleep?

Every night while you're asleep, you move your body about 40 times. You don't move just because you're restless. Every time you move, you help your blood flow through your body. Also, moving around keeps your muscles from getting stiff.

Can I hear while I'm asleep?

Even though most noises won't wake you up, they are still "heard" by your brain. The reason you don't wake up is that your brain decides which sounds are important enough to wake you up. Do you know the one sound that probably will wake you up most of the time? It's the sound of your own name!

Why do I only dream sometimes?

Actually, you dream every night, but you don't always remember your dreams. If you slept ten hours last night, you probably spent about two and a half hours dreaming.

Published in 1995 by Wishing Well Books,
an imprint of Joshua Morris Publishing, Inc.,
355 Riverside Avenue, Westport, CT 06880.
Copyright © 1988 Joshua Morris Publishing, Inc.
All rights reserved. Printed in Hong Kong.
ISBN: 0-88705-622-9
10 9 8 7 6 5 4

WISHING WELL BOOKS & DESIGN is a registered trademark
of The Reader's Digest Association, Inc.